LATIN IN CHURCH

CAMBRIDGE
UNIVERSITY PRESS

University Printing House, Cambridge CB2 8BS, United Kingdom

Cambridge University Press is part of the University of Cambridge.

It furthers the University's mission by disseminating knowledge in the pursuit of education, learning and research at the highest international levels of excellence.

www.cambridge.org
Information on this title: www.cambridge.org/9781107675230

© Cambridge University Press 1934

First published 1934
First paperback edition 2014

A catalogue record for this publication is available from the British Library

ISBN 978-1-107-67523-0 Paperback

Latin in Church

EPISODES IN THE
HISTORY OF ITS PRONUNCIATION
PARTICULARLY IN ENGLAND

BY

F. BRITTAIN, M.A.

Assistant Lecturer and Librarian of
Jesus College, Cambridge

"*Not for any private malice that I bear*
to Italy, which country I have always
specially honoured."   Ascham

CAMBRIDGE
AT THE UNIVERSITY PRESS
1934

To

H. G. COMBER

I

The custom of imitating the Italian pronunciation of Church Latin is unquestionably growing, both on the Continent and in England, among church choirs and among choral societies.

On the Continent, italianisation is by no means universal, even among those who pay ecclesiastical allegiance to Rome. Its growth among the latter is nevertheless understandable, particularly since the introduction of cheap and quick transport and the invention of the wireless. Thousands can now visit Rome who, fifty years ago, would never have left their own country. Millions who, even to-day, cannot afford to visit Rome, can listen to a service broadcast from St Peter's and can hear the Pope himself. Consequently, *Roma locuta est* has acquired a new significance; for, even though Rome has not issued a direct command on the pronunciation of Latin, its example is bound to have considerable effect on its adherents.

The growth of the Italian pronunciation in England, however, is not so understandable, seeing that most Englishmen are outside the papal fold and pride themselves on their insularity. It is least understandable in those of them who, in an attempt to reduce the Roman church in England to its lowest terms, refer to it depreciatingly as "the Italian Mission".

Those of the depreciators who adopt the Italian

pronunciation, however, sometimes comfort themselves with the belief that it is not specifically Italian, but non-national, the peculiar property of the church universal—a pronunciation which somehow has descended, with little or no alteration in any country, from a remote past, when the bishops of Rome had not begun to think of themselves as popes.

Apart from ignorance of philology, there appear to be two causes of this popular impression. The earlier of these is the influence of manuals for singers, in which an Italian pronunciation of Church Latin has been freely recommended for a good many years past, the recommendation being often coupled with a hint that it is the only possible pronunciation for liturgical Latin. The second cause is, as on the Continent, the development of the wireless habit. Many persons who would never attend a Roman Catholic church listen to its services from their homes. As the Latin pronunciation which they hear is an Italian one, the popular belief that the Roman church never changes, and that it is the same everywhere, helps them to jump to the conclusion that the pronunciation which they hear has been used by the church at all times and in all places. Hence it ceases to be to them a mere Italian pronunciation, and becomes "*the* ecclesiastical pronunciation".

The reply to this belief, briefly put, is that there never was a uniform pronunciation of Latin, either ecclesiastical or secular; that there is not *an* ecclesiastical pronunciation of Latin to-day, any more than there is a military one or a medical one; and that the Italian pronunciation was not used in England until the nineteenth century was well advanced.

We will consider these points in order.

II

It is true that, under the Roman Empire, variations in the Latin language were much less evident than they became soon after the empire fell. "Administration and military service", says Professor Grandgent,[1] "tended to obliterate distinctions; under the Empire the variations probably came to be no greater than those now to be found in the English of the British Empire."

Yet, though it is highly probable that there was a remarkable uniformity of language in accidence, syntax, and even vocabulary throughout the empire, it is equally probable that this uniformity did not extend to pronunciation.

Such uniformity, indeed, could not be expected, for Latin was introduced into the various provinces of the empire from different parts of Italy

[1] C. H. Grandgent, *An Introduction to Vulgar Latin.* Boston, Heath, 1907, p. 3.

and at different stages in the development of the language. Further, the empire covered a vast area, and Latin consequently came into contact with many different languages and races. However willingly and rapidly the inhabitants of any particular province may have adopted the Latin tongue, their pronunciation of it was bound to be influenced by their native habits of speech.[1]

We find evidence of diversity of pronunciation throughout the imperial period. In the first century, the pronunciation of Augustus himself distressed the grammarians. In the second century, Hadrian was chaffed for his Spanish accent. The *Appendix Probi* gives some idea of the extent to which variations had grown by the third or fourth century; and St Jerome, writing about the time of the fall of Rome, remarks that *Latinitas ipsa et regionibus quotidie variatur et tempore.*

The expansion of the Christian church after the fall of the empire, far from acting as a check, fostered differentiations of pronunciation which the imperial organisation had retarded. The growth of Christianity, in fact, can be put side by side with the barbarian invasions of the fifth century as one of the two special causes which accelerated the break-up of such phonetic homogeneity as had previously existed.

[1] Cf. A. Darmesteter, *A Historical French Grammar.* London, Macmillan, 1899, p. 8.

It was natural that this should be so; for, although the Fathers of the first five centuries loved the classics and owed their education almost entirely to the pagan public schools, their chief interest in life was not grammar or literature but religion. Correctness of pronunciation can have weighed as nothing with such men as St Jerome—except perhaps as something to get away from. For did he not, in a vision, see himself damned for being a better Ciceronian than Christian?

The ordinary clergy, who were not distinguished for learning and did not possess St Jerome's great love for the classics, must have had even less regard for niceties of speech than he. Faced with the twofold duty of strengthening the faithful and converting the heathen, they wrote in popular Latin, careless of nice points of style, and careful only of writing in such a way as to be easily understood. They soon began to write hymns in popular rhythmical form, disregarding the laws of classical prosody. Above all, in whatever locality they ministered, they adopted the pronunciation of the masses, so as to reach them more easily. If they had not done so, Christianity would have spread much less quickly than it did.

III

The church grew rapidly between the fall of Rome in the year 410 and the coronation of Charlemagne in 800.[1] During this period, the liturgy, formerly fluid, assumed a fixed form; but there is nothing to suggest that a fixed liturgy was accompanied by a fixed pronunciation. Latin was breaking up more and more into regional dialects—the Romance languages in embryo—but Latin of a kind was still the spoken language throughout what had been the Western Empire. The gulf between liturgical Latin and popular Latin continued to widen; but, merely because the church, in its service-books, retained the Latin of the fifth and sixth centuries, we have no reason to assume that it essayed the arduous and unnecessary task of retaining also the pronunciation of that period, or the equally arduous task of revising its pronunciation from time to time to conform with Italian standards.

Even if the clergy had wanted to use an Italian pronunciation of Latin, they would have needed to visit Italy frequently, for pronunciation was no more stable there than elsewhere. The characteristically Italian *chee* sound of *c* before *e* or *i*, for

[1] For a recent study of the Latin language during this period, cf. H. F. Muller and P. Taylor, *A Chrestomathy of Vulgar Latin*, Boston, U.S.A., 1932.

instance, did not develop until the church already possessed a settled liturgy. If, on the other hand, the clergy of any country, including Italy, had clung throughout the centuries to the pronunciation of the early church, they would be saying *Pater noster, qui es in kaelis* to this day.

The fact that they do not do so is but one of many proofs that Latin was not deliberately retained as a hieratic language. It merely became so, by the natural and gradual divergence of the Romance languages from it. The time came when it was necessary to order the clergy to preach in the vernacular, because the laity no longer understood literary Latin; but that was not until the ninth century. Even then, the retention of Latin as the liturgical language was not due to a deliberate intention to use a language which was not "understanded of the people". It was due to mere conservatism, not to principle. The use of Latin became a principle only when the reformers of the sixteenth century and their precursors objected to its continuance.

If no principle was involved in the use of Latin as the liturgical language, still less could there have been any principle about the use of any particular pronunciation. One can admit this without denying the existence, during the Vulgar Latin period, of a clerical accent, whether of liturgical Latin or of popular Latin.

There has no doubt been a clerical accent at all times. To this day, there are Anglican clerics who talk of the epis-tells of St Paul and exhort their congregations to acknōwledge and confess their manifold sins. Such idiosyncrasies, however, are few in number, are not peculiar to the clergy, and are used only by a small fraction of them. The clerical accent undoubtedly exists, but the candid layman will admit that he hears it far less frequently coming from the pulpit or the parson's stall than from the comic stage.

The clergy of the Vulgar Latin period similarly had their little peculiarities of speech. Such evidence as has survived about their Latin pronunciation, however, does not indicate any wide departure from popular usage, nor does it show a predilection for an Italian or any other local accent.[1]

IV

A new situation arose with the opening of the Middle Ages properly so called. The Romance languages were now evolved from popular Latin and gradually produced a literature of their own, leaving Latin stranded as the language of the liturgy, of scholarship, and of diplomacy. Further, the Christian faith now had a firm hold on non-

[1] Cf. Grandgent, *op. cit.* §§ 218, 259 and note 1, 260[1], 276, 277[1], 318 (1), 333 (1).

Romance countries; and, even in Romance countries, the gulf which had formed naturally between vernacular speech and the liturgical language was made still wider by Charlemagne's reforms. He aimed, not merely at the introduction of a purer Latin style than had existed for a long time, but also at the suppression of local rites and their replacement by a uniform Roman rite throughout his dominions. Might not the clergy, faced with this demand for uniformity, have adopted a uniform pronunciation of Latin, introduced from Italy?

If so, how did they get it? The introduction of a uniform rite was a difficult matter and was in fact never wholly accomplished. The introduction of a uniform pronunciation, if anyone tried it, must have been an all but impossible task, in view of the circumstances of the time. Even if we assume that it was attempted and accomplished, it cannot have survived for long.

The descendants of the Norman conquerors tried to keep the Norman-French language alive in England, but failed to keep even its vocabulary alive as an independent language, although they were separated from Normandy merely by the English Channel. The influence of the surrounding English tongue was too much for them. It is true that some Norman-French words managed to survive without being swallowed up in the

English language, and that they survive to this day, with something like their original pronunciation. These survivors, however, are either place-names or words which owe their preservation to their being used in isolated formulas, generally by persons who have not understood their meaning.

Attempts to keep an Italian or an archaic pronunciation of Latin alive among the scattered clergy of Europe must have encountered at least as much difficulty. In Romance-speaking countries, the difficulty would have been even greater than elsewhere, owing to the close affinity between Latin and the vernacular. This affinity must have made the assimilation of Latin pronunciation to the local Romance pronunciation almost inevitable.

The history of one or two Norman-French words in England illustrates this point. The final consonant in *Rievaulx* has been sounded in English since Rievaulx Abbey was founded in 1131, and has been preserved to this day in the local pronunciation *Rivvaz*. So many Englishmen, however, now know some modern French that Rievaulx is being rapidly transferred to quasi-Romance territory, and is being called *Ree-vo*. The old pronunciation will probably disappear in a few years. The town-criers of England, who know no French, have similarly perpetuated the medieval pronunciation of the imperative *Oyez!* in their *Oh-yez!* and *Oh-yes!* The pageant-producer, however, who knows some (but not enough) French, and scorns the town-crier as an ignoramus, insists on calling it *Oi-yay!*[1]

It may be urged, however, that it is unfair to quote the fate of the Norman-French language, as, unlike Latin, it was not protected by liturgical usage, which is notoriously conservative.

It will be readily admitted that liturgical language changes more slowly than non-liturgical language, but the admission must be coupled with an important reservation—viz. that the retardation is very much greater in vocabulary than in phonetics.

Archaism of vocabulary is obvious, for instance, in almost every line of the Book of Common Prayer, even in its 1928 revision; but the phonetic archaisms when its contents are said or sung are very few in number, and are practically limited to such parts of the book as are sung. They amount to little more than the use of *wīnd* for *wind*, the pronunciation of final *-ed* as a separate syllable in such words as *avenged*, and the use of

---

[1] His example was followed in 1932 by a competitor in the town-criers' contest at Lyme Regis. One suspects that those who know some modern French will not rest until they have induced the farm-labourer to call his mid-morning *beever*—or *bayver*, as it is called in Bedfordshire— his *boire*.

an archaic pronunciation of certain Hebrew personal names.[1]

Even "extreme" Anglican clergymen, who are not unfavourable to a hieratic language, are satisfied with Ah-braham, Dah-vid, and the vex-ed wĭnd. The average Anglican cleric does not try to make the language of the Prayer Book more unintelligible than it is on paper. When he has compelled a bridegroom to say: "and thereto I plight thee my troth", he does not increase the confusion by reading the rest of the service with a sixteenth-century accent. Besides, not one parson in a thousand could do so, even if he wished.

The medieval parson had no more reason than his modern successor to increase the confusion of his parishioners unnecessarily. He used Latin, it is true; but conservation of an archaic language did not bind him to use an archaic or an alien pronunciation. Neither had he more knowledge than the parson of to-day if he wished to use such a pronunciation. He had, indeed, very much less.

Here and there, no doubt, a travelled cleric

[1] Abraham, for instance, who is called Ay-braham in ordinary speech, generally becomes Ah-braham in the psalms, but reverts to Ay-braham in the lessons. It is most probable, too, that this archaic pronunciation of Hebrew names is merely a learned re-introduction, dating only from the nineteenth century.

used a foreign pronunciation. Clerics of to-day who have just returned from an Italian holiday are not unknown to dwell on their experiences in their sermons, and even to introduce a few Italian words into them. So, perhaps, the medieval cleric who had visited Rome did not fail to let his parishioners know it by his manner of singing the Mass when he returned. Yet it is probable that then, as now, the returned traveller was as immersed in parochialism as ever within a few weeks.

Taking all these points into consideration, and linking them with evidence from the early sixteenth century and from current Continental practice, we feel justified in concluding that the medieval clergy, taken as a whole, pronounced Latin in accordance with the phonetic principles of their native language, though they may always have been fifty years or more behind the rest of the community in adopting phonetic changes.

V

Nevertheless, the belief persists that there was a uniform pronunciation of Church Latin throughout the Middle Ages, until the Reformation—so often credited with destroying the marvellous unity of medieval Europe—came and swept it away. Some believe this as firmly as others believe that the sea-serpent exists or that a ray of sunlight will infallibly put a fire out.

Sir Rennell Rodd, for instance, in a letter published in a London newspaper early in 1932, wrote as follows:

"Surely"—and his prefixing this word prepares the reader for a controvertible statement—"surely there can be little doubt that for a considerable time after the establishment of the reformed religion in England the old ecclesiastical pronunciation of Latin, with which educated people were familiar, remained in general use."

He then proceeds to speak of "the old ecclesiastical pronunciation" in terms which show that he identifies it with the Italian pronunciation, and commends the adoption of the latter as a "simple solution of the problem" of international pronunciation of Latin at the present day. It was by means of "the ecclesiastical pronunciation", he asserts, that Queen Elizabeth and the Polish ambassador readily understood one another when conversing together in Latin.

Yet, merely because they understood one another, one is not justified in concluding that they used the same pronunciation. A Scotchman and a Welshman can carry on a conversation in English, and understand one another, though they are using very different pronunciations. A Spaniard and an Italian can carry on a conversation together, each in his own language, and understand one another, even though they are using, not merely different pronunciations, but also different languages. The anecdote about the queen and the ambassador certainly does not prove that Latin was pronounced in the same way, or even in anything approaching the same way, in all European countries, ecclesiastically or otherwise. It would indeed have been remarkable if there had been identity of pronunciation in the sixteenth century, in two non-Latin countries as widely separated as England and Poland, seeing how greatly Latin pronunciation had varied in its own territory—the different provinces of the empire—a thousand years before, and to how many different neo-Latin tongues those variations of pronunciation had given birth.

Let us, however, for the sake of argument, assume that an international pronunciation of Latin, having surmounted every obstacle to its existence throughout the Dark Ages and the Middle Ages, surmounted also the Reformation. Let us assume that this pronunciation survived into Elizabeth's reign, even in Protestant England.

If we assume that it existed in Elizabeth's reign, we must *a fortiori* assume that it existed in the reign of Henry VIII. No doubt, therefore, we shall find a good deal about it in one of the less-known works of Erasmus—his *De recta*

Latini Graecique sermonis pronuntiatione, published in 1528.

Yet, when we examine this interesting work, which takes the form of a dialogue between "Ursus" and "Leo", we find that its chief theme is a lament on the complete absence of any international pronunciation. Part of the confusion, says "Ursus", is due to natural defects of the speech-organs; but more of it is due to negligence or affectation, and a large part of it to the practice of the various nations—Spain, Italy, France, Germany, and England, for instance—of pronouncing Latin in their own way. A little later, he asserts that practically all pronunciation, of both Greek and Latin, is corrupt, partly because vulgar speech itself is corrupt, and partly because sounds cannot be expressed in writing.

Numerous examples are given in the Dialogue of contemporary pronunciations of Latin. As one might expect, many of these are chosen from Holland; but Erasmus takes full advantage of his extensive travels and cosmopolitan friendships to illustrate his points. Consequently, the space which he gives to peculiarities of pronunciation due to natural defects or affectation is small compared with that which he devotes to national pronunciations.

The feature which perhaps strikes one most in the examples which he gives is always the same, i.e. that the various national pronunciations of Latin reproduce the phonetic peculiarities of the vernacular.

The French, for instance, pronounce Latin *u* in their own peculiar way, and prefix an *e* to words beginning with *st* and *sp*. Thus they say *esto* for *sto*, and *especto* for *specto*. The Germans adopt the French *u rotundiore mugitu*, the Westphalians doing so to an extreme degree. They confuse *b* and *p*, saying *pipere* for *bibere*, and *biper* for *piper*. Some of the Dutch affect the Westphalian *u*, but are not very successful in doing so. Their *c* before *e* and *i* is practically identical with *s*, and it is impossible to tell whether they are saying *coenae* or *sene*. Some of the Spaniards, like the French, prefix *e* to initial *sp* and *st*, and confuse *b* and *v*, saying *bibit* for *vivit*.[1]

The Italians, too, though they are given qualified praise for distinguishing between the sounds of *s* and *c* before *e* or *i*, and—contrary to their practice to-day—for not giving a *z* sound to intervocalic *s*, do not escape criticism. Some of them, for instance, affect the French *u*. Others say *laldo* for *laudo*, and *aldio* for *audio*. At Rome

---

[1] English travellers in Spain to-day are occasionally entertained by seeing the word *bino* painted over a wineshop instead of *vino*. The invocation of Spain as *Felix natio, ubi vivere est bibere* is probably based on Lipsius's description of Spaniards as *homines sobrii et quibus non placet bibere sed vivere*.

itself, says "Ursus"—who is to be identified with Erasmus—he had heard priests singing *degus* for *deus,* and *egum* or *echum* for *eum.*

Equidem arbitrabar nos solos barbaros sonare barbare, says "Leo".

Hodie vulgus nusquam non est barbarum, replies "Ursus".

Erasmus seldom differentiates between clerical and lay pronunciation of Latin; but, whenever he specifies the former, it is to condemn it. In particular, he attributes the confusion of long syllables with short syllables largely to the bad example of the clergy. If a man wants to know what is meant by a short syllable, says "Ursus", let him listen to Carthusians rattling through the psalms on feast-days, making all syllables short. If he wants to know what a long syllable is, monks of more austere observance will provide him with an unbroken sequence of spondees.

Towards the end of the dialogue, "Ursus" relates an anecdote which gives an admirable picture of the state of Latin pronunciation throughout Europe at the time. It is much more valuable than the story of Queen Elizabeth and the Polish ambassador.

Not long before, he says, the Emperor Maximilian gave an audience to the ambassadors of several countries. The French ambassador, who was a native of Maine, made a complimentary speech which had been written for him, probably by an Italian. The speech was in Latin, but was delivered with so Gallic an accent that the Italians present thought he was speaking French, and he was several times interrupted by bursts of laughter. A German, a member of the Aulic Council, who was called upon to reply, made an extemporary speech, and began thus: *Caesarea maghestas pene caudet fidere vos, et horationem festram lipenter audifit.* His pronunciation, says "Ursus", was so Germanic that it could not have been more so if he had been speaking German, and he evoked even more laughter than the Frenchman. A Dane who spoke third might have been a Scotchman, as marvellously did he reproduce the pronunciation of Scotland. A Dutchman followed him, and one could have sworn that neither of these two was speaking Latin.

Now these orators were all educated men, and must have been familiar with "the old ecclesiastical pronunciation", if there was one. Why then, did they not use it, and so avoid the laughter which nettled some of them? The reason is obvious.

VI

The chaotic state of Latin pronunciation throughout Europe, whether in church or out of church, led Erasmus to a conclusion to which his tastes also led him, i.e. that the only remedy was to return to the pronunciation of classical times. A considerable part of his Dialogue is devoted to discussing what this pronunciation was, and his conclusions are to a large extent identical with what is now called the new or reformed classical pronunciation. He wants *c*, for instance, to be pronounced as *k*, no matter what vowel follows.

His suggested pronunciation would no doubt have been welcomed by many of the leading churchmen of the time—in particular, by Cardinal Bembo, who declared that he could not read the Breviary, for by doing so he might spoil his Latin style.

Yet it is probable that little or nothing was done to introduce a uniform pronunciation of Church Latin, whether on Erasmus's lines or on any others; for, from the point of view both of Renaissance scholarship and of uniformity, there was much more important work to be done, viz. the reform of the vocabulary and syntax of the liturgy, and the enforcement of a single rite to replace the existing welter of local rites.

The first of these objects took some time to carry out. It was not until 1570 that a revised Roman Missal was published, from which nearly all the sequences and other features offensive to Renaissance ears had been swept out. It was another sixty years before a revised Breviary appeared, with most of its office hymns either touched up or re-written to conform with the laws of classical prosody and vocabulary.

Uniformity of rite took much longer to achieve. Many local uses were suppressed before the end of the sixteenth century, but it was not until the second half of the nineteenth century that, owing to the gradual dropping of Gallican and German uses, the Roman use was left virtually the sole survivor of all the Latin rites.

Yet, although it was about three hundred years after the Council of Trent before liturgical uniformity was secured, that time was short compared with what would have been needed to secure uniformity of pronunciation. If any such attempt was ever made—and that is most unlikely—it had been abandoned by 1870, and the clergy had returned to their old habit of pronouncing Latin like the vernacular.

It may possibly be argued that Erasmus, who hated fish and declared that he had a Protestant stomach, may also have had a Protestant ear. Might he not, with his predilection for the pronunciation of pagan times, have selected from the available evidence only such facts as tended to show the non-existence of a uniform pronunciation which was in existence all the time?

The possession of a Protestant ear, however,

can scarcely be attributed to the great company of ecclesiastics who came to Rome from all over the world to take part in the Vatican Council in 1870. Railways, moreover, had been in general use for some years, so that communication with Rome had for some time been vastly easier than ever before.

Even so, uniformity of pronunciation was not expected at the Council. Reporters, in fact, had been specially trained to record the speeches of ecclesiastics with French, Spanish, and other national pronunciations of Latin.[1]

Nor were they trained for nothing, for such pronunciations were freely used. Yet, like Queen Elizabeth and the Polish ambassador, the speakers understood one another. Only once, in fact, does there appear to have been serious difficulty in this respect. This was when the Bishop of Poitiers —a zealous Ultramontane, it is interesting to note —was making a lengthy speech in Latin, with a French pronunciation. "Some Italian bishops called out that they could not understand. He repeated a sentence slowly in his best Italian style, and then said: *Gallus sum, et Gallice loquor.*"[2]

The outcome of the Vatican Council was an increased centralisation of the Latin church on

---

[1] Dom Cuthbert Butler, *The Vatican Council*, vol. 1. London, Longmans, 1930, p. 291, n. 1.

[2] Butler, *op. cit.* p. 192. Cf. also p. 191.

the papacy, and the spread of the Italian pronunciation of Latin may be regarded as one of its by-products. Its dissemination received considerable impetus with the accession of Pius X, who was Pope from 1903 to 1914. An ardent advocate of the restoration of Gregorian music, he warmly commended the adoption of the Italian pronunciation of Latin as a useful ally in the cause. His sentiments on the subject are summed up in a letter[1] which he addressed to the Archbishop of Bourges in 1912.

In this letter, he expresses his pleasure at the advance of the Italian pronunciation in France since the promulgation of his *Motu proprio* on sacred music in 1904. The question of the pronunciation of Latin, he says, is intimately connected with the cause of Gregorian music. The adoption of the Italian pronunciation in France will help to consolidate the liturgical unity of France brought about by its adoption of the Roman liturgy. Consequently, he hopes that the movement to adopt the Roman pronunciation will continue "avec le même zèle et les mêmes succès consolants qui ont marqué jusqu'à présent sa marche progressive".

It was only natural if Pius X's remarks were taken to heart in other countries than France,

[1] Text in *Actes de S.S. Pie X*, tome VII. Paris, Bonne Presse, no date [? 1920], p. 168–9.

and it is highly probable that his letter led to a considerable adoption of the Italian pronunciation in various parts of Europe.

At the same time, his commendation was not a command, and none of his successors in the papacy has made it so. Consequently, if we examine European practice to-day, we still find considerable diversity, among ecclesiastics as among laymen. In spite of Pius X's letter, in spite of the introduction of gramophones, aeroplanes, and even the wireless, national pronunciations of Latin still thrive in liturgical use. Where Ultramontanism is not triumphant—and sometimes even there—ecclesiastics generally pronounce Latin like their own vernacular. A French priest reciting the *Gloria Patri*, for instance, will say: *Sicüt erat in prĕsipio*; a Spanish priest will announce the Gospel as *Inithium sancti ebanhelii*; a German priest will end the Lord's Prayer with *in zaecula zaeculorum*; and a Portuguese cantor will sing *Adeshtɔ, fidelesh*.

"I have been reminded", says Sir Rennell Rodd in the letter already quoted, "when advocating this simple solution of the problem, that Continental nations do not all pronounce Latin exactly alike. Shades of difference may exist, but they are so slight as to be negligible."

Would he maintain that the examples quoted above are but slight variations from Italian pronunciation?[1] If he asserts that he can follow the Mass, word for word, in any country of the Latin rite, his experience has been very different from that of a certain English professor, a practising Roman Catholic, with an intimate knowledge of several European languages, including French and Italian. This professor laments that, whenever he has heard a Frenchman giving a mere Latin quotation, he has never understood a word of it, owing to the absence of stress-accent and the disfigurement of the Latin by the French phrase-accent.

The French pronunciation of Latin, however, is an extreme case, for it is notoriously in a class by itself. Disregarding it for the moment, there is in the contention that Continental nations pronounce Latin more or less in the same way this element of truth, viz. that their pronunciations fall into one class, whereas English pronunciation stands in a separate class, further from them than even the French pronunciation stands. We will next consider how the great difference between the English pronunciation and the various Continental pronunciations has arisen.

[1] Professor H. J. Rose, writing in *The Times* on January 23, 1934, says "The pronunciation of Latin used in the Church of Rome is probably not far removed from St Augustine's." Which of the numerous pronunciations used in the Church of Rome does he mean?

VII

There is no doubt that English pronunciation of Latin immediately before the Reformation differed considerably from what is to-day, in contradistinction to the reformed classical pronunciation, called the "old" pronunciation. The latter is thoroughly insular, utterly different from any Continental pronunciation. Up to the Reformation, on the other hand, the English pronunciation of Latin was considerably nearer to the Continental type. How is our modern insularity to be explained?

Some—including a learned Jesuit—explain it by what might be called a philological *Nag's Head* story. Just as it has at various times been asserted that, in order to make a complete break with pre-Reformation times, an entirely new line of bishops was started in Queen Elizabeth's reign by deliberately uncanonical procedure in a Fleet Street public-house, so it is asserted that English scholars deliberately smashed the pre-Reformation pronunciation of Latin and replaced it by a new, insular, Protestant, and purely artificial pronunciation.

The contention is a plausible one. After all, did not the English reformers deliberately smash some of the links which had bound the religion and culture of their country with the greater part of Europe? Were they not intent on fostering the nationalist character of the Church of England in every possible way? Would it not be perfectly natural, therefore, it they deliberately started a fresh pronunciation of Latin?

Philological evidence, however, does not support this argument. On the contrary, there is both direct and indirect evidence to contradict it.

In the first place, as we have seen, there was no Catholic or pan-European pronunciation of Latin from which England needed to break away in order to assert its independence. Further, while it is true that English pronunciation of Latin was nearer the average Continental type than it is to-day, yet it is clear from Erasmus's *Dialogus* that in 1528 Latin was pronounced in England on national lines.

Erasmus certainly praises English pronunciation of Latin highly. He remarks that the Italians regard it as being, next to their own, the most correct pronunciation in use at the time, and he puts the French pronunciation at the bottom of the scale from his classical point of view.

At the same time, he criticises the English pronunciation. He notes, for instance, English attempts to imitate objectionable features of Continental pronunciations—the extreme Westphalian *u*, for instance. He had frequently heard priests in the British Isles affecting this sound, he says, but their attempts were no more successful than those of the Dutch.

As an instance of the effect of the vernacular on the pronunciation of Latin, he notes that some of the Scotch almost turn *e* into *i*, saying *faciibat* for *faciebat*. The same peculiarity is noticed as used by one of the best English scholars of the time. This is John Colet, *vir alioqui facundus et eruditus*, who had followed this bad practice from boyhood, and could not be broken of it, either in speech or in writing, although reproved by his friends. As we know, this conversion of long *e* from its old sound to its modern *ee* sound ultimately became universal in the English pronunciation of Latin, and the same change has been made in the corresponding English vowel in most words in which it occurs.

Less than ten years after the publication of Erasmus's *Dialogus*, two young Cambridge scholars, Thomas Smith and John Cheke, began to introduce into the university a reformed pronunciation of Greek and Latin, based largely on his theories.[1] In 1540 they were elected to two

[1] Cf. Thomas Smith, *De recta et emendata linguae Graecae pronuntiatione*, Paris, 1542; John Cheke, *De pronuntiatione Graecae potissimum linguae*, Basiliae, 1555; John Strype, *Life of Sir John Cheke*, London, 1705; J. E. Sandys, *History of Classical Scholarship*, 3 vols. Cambridge, 1903–8.

of the Regius professorships founded in that year. They continued to use the new pronunciation, but the opposition which it had aroused from the first did not subside, and in 1542 the Chancellor of the University, Stephen Gardiner, issued a decree condemning it. "Let no one who recognises my authority", he says, "dare to affix, to Greek or Latin letters, sounds which differ from the public usage of the present time."

Smith's reply to Gardiner, published in the same year, shows that the usual English pronunciation of Latin, though closely allied to the Italian pronunciation, was distinctly national. "When I was in France", he says, "I deferred to their extremely corrupt pronunciation of Latin. When I was in Italy, I pronounced certain letters in the Italian way. When I returned home, I was satisfied with our method of pronunciation." He could understand an Italian speaking Latin, he says, with the greatest ease, but he could not understand a Frenchman.

Gardiner's decree, however, was not strictly enforced until 1554. It was abandoned at the accession of Elizabeth four years later, when the Erasmian pronunciation of Greek came into general use in England. Whether or no the Erasmian pronunciation of Latin was adopted at the same time, there are no instructions for its use in the *Brevissima Institutio* appended, at some date not later than 1569, to the celebrated work commonly known as *Lily's Latin Grammar*, which long remained the standard work of its kind for English schools. The *Institutio* is concerned merely with eradicating peculiarities of pronunciation due to the influence of English dialects or French.[1]

Lipsius's treatise on Latin pronunciation, published in 1586, provides at least one useful piece of evidence on the English pronunciation of Latin towards the end of the sixteenth century.[2] The English, he says, pronounce *regina, amicus,* and *vita* as *regeina, ameicus,* and *veita*. In other words, the sound of the Latin long *i* was following the changes in the English long *i* which have gradually brought it to its present sound.

A passage in the *Merry Wives of Windsor*,[3] written about the year 1600, provides a little further evidence of contemporary English—and also Welsh clerical—pronunciation of Latin, showing how closely the vernacular was followed:

MRS PAGE. Sir Hugh, my husband says my son profits nothing in the world at his book: I pray you, ask him some questions in his accidence.

EVANS. Come hither, William; hold up your head; come....What is *fair*, William?

---

[1] Cf. H. M. Ayres, "A Note on the School Pronunciation of Latin in England", *Speculum*, vol. 1 (1926), pp. 440–3, where the text of the *Institutio* is reprinted.

[2] Lipsius, *De recta pronuntiatione Latinae linguae dialogus*, 1586. Edition Antwerp, 1628, p. 23.   [3] Act IV, Scene 1.

WILLIAM. *Pulcher.*

MRS QUICKLY. Polecats! there are fairer things than polecats, sure.

EVANS. ...What is he, William, that does lend articles?

WILLIAM. Articles are borrowed of the pronoun, and be thus declined, *Singulariter, nominativo, hic, haec, hoc.*

EVANS. *Nominativo, hig, hag, hog...accusativo, hung, hang, hog.*

MRS QUICKLY. Hang hog is Latin for bacon, I warrant you.

EVANS. Remember, William; focative is *caret.*

MRS QUICKLY. And that's a good root.

WILLIAM. ...*Genitivo, horum, harum, horum.*

MRS QUICKLY. You do ill to teach the child such words. He teaches him to hick and to hack, which they'll do fast enough of themselves, and to cry "horum". Fie upon you!

By 1608, the English pronunciation of Latin had diverged still further from Continental types. Scaliger, who received a visit from some unknown Englishman at Leyden in that year, listened to a lengthy Latin discourse from his visitor; but, not even recognising it as Latin, he brought the speech to a close by expressing his regret at being unable to understand English very well.

Thomas Coryat, who toured the Continent in the same year, found, wherever he went, that the sound of long *i* was utterly different from that used in England. "Whereupon", he says, "having observed such a generall consent amongst them in the pronunciation of this letter, I have thought good to imitate these nations herein, and to abandon my old English pronunciation of *vita*, *fides*, and *amicus*, as being utterly dissonant from the sound of all other Nations; and have determined (God willing) to retayne the same till my dying day."[1]

By the middle of the seventeenth century, the gulf between the English pronunciation of Latin and Continental pronunciations had grown wider still. Milton refers to it in his treatise *Of Education*, published in 1644. In view of his taste for things Italian, it is not surprising that he takes the Italian pronunciation as a model. He advises teachers of Latin to encourage "a distinct and clear pronunciation, as near as may be to the Italian, especially in the Vowels. For we Englishmen, being far Northerly, do not open our mouths in the cold air wide enough to grace a Southern Tongue; but are observ'd by all other Nations to speak exceeding close and inward; so that to smatter Latin with an English mouth is as ill a-hearing as Law-French".

His efforts, however, apparently met with little success; for, writing in 1661, he remarks that

---

[1] Thomas Coryat, *Crudities*, 1611. Edition Glasgow, 1905, vol. II, p. 60.

"few will be perswaded to pronounce Latin otherwise than their own English".[1]

Evidence about the pronunciation of Latin in England during the eighteenth century is difficult to find, but fortunately there is no need to trace its history in detail, for we know what it had become by the nineteenth century and what it still is to-day. Since the time of Erasmus, it has followed the changes in English phonetics step by step.

As Professor Postgate says:[2] "Everyone who has even a slight acquaintance with the history of our language knows that the sounds of the English language have changed enormously since the introduction of Latin into our schools, but that the spelling has remained where it was. And since English and Latin are written in the same alphabet, the pronunciation of the letters in Latin has followed the change of their pronunciation in English".

The change from the medieval English pronunciation of Latin to the modern pronunciation was therefore a perfectly natural development, with nothing artificial about it. The Italians of Erasmus's time praised the English pronuncia-

[1] Milton, *Accedence commenc'd Grammar*, 1661. Edition London, 1738, vol. I, p. 607.

[2] J. P. Postgate, *How to Pronounce Latin*. London, Bell, 1907, p. 4. Professor Postgate's subject is limited to the pronunciation of Classical Latin.

tion, not because it was a deliberate imitation of their own, but because the vowel-symbols, in English speech and consequently in the English pronunciation of Latin, were still given sounds roughly corresponding to those which the Italians gave them. On the whole, English vowels were still pure, whereas French vowels had already undergone revolutionary changes through nasalisation.

Since the Reformation, English consonants have changed comparatively little, but the vowels have suffered great changes, so that some of the symbols have practically exchanged sounds with each other. On the Continent, on the other hand, these changes have not gone so far. The result is that, in the various Continental pronunciations of Latin, the vowels, which are the most important factor, still bear a recognisable resemblance to each other, but are utterly different from the English vowels.

The philological *Nag's Head* should therefore be consigned to oblivion with the liturgical *Nag's Head*, or even before it; for the modern English pronunciation of Latin can be attributed to deliberate Protestantism only if we ascribe all the changes in English phonetics to the same cause. Evidence from the early years of the nineteenth century supports this conclusion.

VIII

In the sixteenth century, English long vowels and the corresponding short vowels were still sufficiently alike to count as rhymes. By the beginning of the nineteenth century, however, most of the long vowels had been radically transformed, whereas most of the short vowels had changed but little.

Long *a*, for instance, had abandoned its former *ah* sound in most words, and had taken on the *ay* sound of the old *e*; but short *a* had not changed much. Long *e*, though it kept its old *ay* sound in such words as *sea* until late in the eighteenth century, had gradually assumed the *ee* sound of the old long *i*; but short *e* had not changed. Long *i* in its turn had changed from its former *ee* sound to its modern diphthongal *eye* sound; but short *i* had stayed where it was.

Consequently, by the beginning of the nineteenth century, Medieval Latin rhymes between short vowels and long vowels would have disappeared if they had been given their current English sounds; for instance, in

> *Dies irae, dies illa,*
> *Solvet saeclum in favilla.*

This difficulty would not have affected the classical scholars of the time, with their lofty

39

disregard of Medieval Latin in general and o rhyming verse in particular. It is important, however, to consider what was the practice of those Englishmen who had to sing Medieval Latin verse regularly. There were such persons, even though they were at the time so insignificant that they might easily be overlooked—the clergy of the Roman obedience.

"But", the pursuers of philological will-o'-the-wisps may say, "surely they need not be considered? Surely they were using the Italian, 'the ecclesiastical' pronunciation?" The answer is that they were not.

"But at least", it may be urged, "surely they were not using the absurd English pronunciation, with its Anglican taint? Or, if they were using it, surely they now abandoned it, lock, stock, and barrel, in favour of the Italian pronunciation—the only one, according to manuals for singers, which is suited to singing?"

The answer to these questions is that they were using the absurd English pronunciation, but that they were giving their vowels something of a Continental sound—just enough, apparently, to preserve the medieval rhymes. They kept to English sounds for the consonants. Their declared aim was "Continental vowels with English consonants", but even their vowels "had an unmistakable Anglo-Saxon sound about them, and would hardly have been recognised on the Continent".[1] To this practice, as we shall see, they clung, until they were forced to abandon it by those who might have been expected to foster its retention. Italianisation was the last thing they wanted.

IX

When we find that the Roman Catholic clergy of England, in the early years of the nineteenth century, aimed at giving their Latin vowels a Continental sound, even if they were not very successful in doing so, it is easy to jump to the conclusion that they were deliberately imitating foreign practice, to that extent at least. Who, one might plausibly argue, would be more likely to do so than men who, until the closing years of the eighteenth century, had perforce received their ecclesiastical training in foreign seminaries—men, moreover, who upheld a religion proscribed by the State, a religion with its headquarters at Rome?

Yet it is quite probable that they were not doing anything of the kind. The vowel-sounds in question were roughly the same as English

---

[1] Monsignor Bernard Ward, *The Sequel to Catholic Emancipation*, vol. II. London, Longmans, 1915, p. 263, note. On what follows, cf. Ward, *op. cit.* pp. 18–20, 92, 236–78.

vowels of an earlier period; and it is highly probable that their use of them represents a conservation of earlier English sounds rather than an imitation of current foreign sounds.

Is not this theory, it may be asked, contrary to what has been already claimed about liturgical usage during the Middle Ages—viz. that it preserved vocabulary and accidence, but did not preserve pronunciation, and could scarcely have done so if it had wished?

The two cases, however, are very different. In the first place, the period from the fall of Rome to the Reformation covered eleven hundred years, but from the Reformation to the beginning of the nineteenth century was less than three hundred years. Again, before the Reformation, Latin was the liturgical language in every church in England, and its pronunciation was bound to be influenced by changes in English phonetics. After the Reformation, liturgical Latin in England became a secret language, and its use was confined to a small, isolated body of men. These men, it is true, were educated abroad, but their seminaries were English enclaves on foreign soil, where they clung to the traditions of their sixteenth-century founders.

A small religious minority is apt to cling to ways of speech which a religious majority discards. The Quakers, for instance, were still saying *thou* and *thee* when the rest of England was saying *you*. From the sixteenth century till near the end of the eighteenth, the Roman Catholic clergy of England possessed the characteristics of a small religious minority to an extraordinary degree, worshipping in holes and corners, and trained by men who had had the same experience. It would not be remarkable if such men preserved, to a great extent, the sixteenth-century pronunciation of Latin vowels down to the nineteenth century, and called the sounds "Continental" merely because that was the most convenient name to give them.

The supposition that they did so is very much strengthened if we consider the general characteristics of English Roman Catholics of the period, and their ecclesiastical habits in particular, before converts began to join them in any considerable numbers.

Perhaps their most striking features were their strong conservatism and their thoroughly English ways. It was, in fact, their constant endeavour to show how English they were. They were prepared to go as far in this direction as it was possible to go without sacrificing their religious principles.

In the closing years of the previous century, for instance, the whole body of them had even denied the doctrine of papal infallibility publicly, while some had demanded a hierarchy in quasi-independence of Rome. There is a flavour of Protestant Dissent about their habit of referring to themselves as "the body"; and, even after the Relief Act of 1791 granted them freedom of worship, they built chapels in the ordinary English style of the day, which is now sometimes termed contemptuously "the Dissenting style of architecture"—plain square buildings with sash-windows, galleries running round three sides of the interior, and high-perched pulpits.

Their devotional practices and language would undoubtedly be scorned by the extreme Anglo-Catholics of to-day and condemned by them as "frightfully Protestant".

They were accustomed to say, for instance, not that they were going to Mass, but—for the memory of penal days was still very fresh—merely that they were going to prayers. Their churches were very plainly furnished, with only one altar. Statues of the Virgin were unknown in them. There were, it is true, pictures of her fairly often; but any veneration of them, whether by burning candles in front of them, or by kneeling before them in prayer, was shunned as un-English and as bordering on superstition. Such services as Benediction were rarely cele-brated. The chief hagiographical work used was Alban Butler's *Lives of the Saints*, and the chief manual of devotions and layman's vade-mecum was Bishop Challoner's *Garden of the Soul*. This was a far more sober work than many Anglican manuals of to-day, and had made such an impress on the minds and ways of the hereditary Roman Catholics that the more advanced converts of post-Emancipation days were accustomed to describe them, and such converts as followed their conservative ways, as "*Garden-of-the-Soul* Catholics".

It would not be surprising, therefore, to find that such men clung to an old-fashioned, insular pronunciation of Latin. Their consonants were avowedly English; and it is reasonable to conclude that their vowels, with their "unmistakable Anglo-Saxon sound", though styled Continental, were survivors from earlier English practice. This remained the pronunciation of the great majority until after the establishment of territorial sees in 1850.

X

There were, it is true, some clerics, educated at Rome, who had already adopted the Italian pronunciation; but its general introduction into England, and its introduction in its extreme form, it is interesting to note, was the work of men not educated at Rome. It was a by-product of the Oxford Movement, being deliberately

45

brought about by those Anglican clerics who seceded to Rome in 1845 or shortly afterwards.

The explanation of this phenomenon is that the new men had all the excessive zeal that distinguishes many converts. Convinced that they had not been Catholics while they were Anglicans, they began to wonder whether the men whom they had joined were Catholics either. They seemed so different from themselves, who had been to Rome—so unable to realise that what was Roman was Catholic, and that what was non-Roman was non-Catholic.

Consequently, although the converts disliked the epithet "Roman" when it was applied to them by Anglicans, they acted in a way which only attached it more firmly to themselves. Not content with being romanisers themselves, they were intent on romanising also the "old Catholics", whom they regarded as an uneducated body and little better than Gallicans. Their insularity and conservatism were to be undermined at all costs.

Conspicuous among the converts was F. W. Faber, who taught people to address the Virgin as "dear mamma", and criticised Alban Butler's *Lives of the Saints* for not giving enough prominence to miracles. Butler, he said, wrote like a Protestant. Other converts, in their yearning to be as un-English and as Italian as possible, talked freely at the altar itself, spat on the floor of the church, allowed dogs to run about it, and in general caused Pugin—himself a convert—to denounce their "admiration of everything debased and modern and trumpery". To convince the world that there was no taint of Anglicanism left in them, they scandalised the hereditary Roman Catholics by referring to the church of their former allegiance as "Mother Damnable" and its clergy as "bonzes".

It need hardly be said that the Latin pronunciation of the hereditary Roman Catholics, with its English consonants and its vowels with "an unmistakable Anglo-Saxon sound", was anathema to such men as these. Nothing less than the Italian pronunciation, the pronunciation of the Pope himself, was good enough for them. Accordingly, with the same zeal with which they introduced "calico hangings, sparkling lustres, paper pots, wax dolls, flounces and furbelows"[1] as ornaments of the church, they set about the introduction of a pronunciation "with an extreme Roman accent".[2] *Caeli*, formerly beginning with an *s* sound, was now to begin with a *ch*; *agnus* was to become *ah-nyoos*; *suscepit* was to be *soo-shay-peet*; *etiam* was to be *ay-tsee-ahm*, and *benedicimus* was to be *bay-nay-dee-chee-moos*.

[1] Pugin, *Treatise on Chancel Screens and Rood Lofts*. London, 1851, p. 101.   [2] Ward, *op. cit.* p. 272.

47

It is little wonder that the hereditary Roman Catholics regarded the whole thing as a nostrum —or, as they perhaps ought to have said, *naustroom*—and that they fought against this alien innovation, holding it up to ridicule under the expressive nickname of "chees and chaws".

The controversy which followed was considerable, and the old pronunciation took some time to die. But, in proportion as Exposition was introduced in spite of the objection that it was unsuitable to England, in proportion as the old chapels in "the Dissenting style of architecture" gave way to cheap imitations of Italian baroque, in proportion as the movement grew "to cut up Gothic vestments to the Roman shape, and to pick off the ornamentation in order to substitute cheap yellow trimmings", in proportion as the convert Cardinal Manning declared that everything Gothic was bound up with Protestantism, so the "chees and chaws" pronunciation spread, supplanting the older and simpler pronunciation in place after place.

Centuries of proscription, isolation, and enforced foreign education had but made the hereditary Roman Catholics more and more determined to stick to English ways. Toleration came in 1791 and brought converts in its train; but still "the body" clung to its insular habits, and its members continued, even among themselves, to refer to their clergy, even their bishops, as plain "Mr". Emancipation came in 1829, and—was it merely a coincidence?—was followed by a stream of converts from those who had stayed outside in penal days and who, even in toleration days, had been no more than a trickle. A few years of emancipation sufficed to blow the insularity of Roman Catholicism in England sky-high, and to convert it into a body which, in language as in devotion and ceremonial, deserved the title of "the Italian Mission" in a way in which it had never deserved it before. It is paradoxical that this transformation was the work, not of the foreign monks who, during the Revolution, had found a refuge in Protestant England from the fury of Catholic France, but of ex-Anglicans, educated at English universities.

Here and there, however, the old pronunciation of Latin managed to retain a footing, and is not extinct even yet.

Among the English Benedictines it survived at Downside until late in the nineteenth century. Latin was pronounced there as though it were English, except that *ā*, *ē*, and *ī* were given their Continental or earlier English sounds. No attempt was made, however, to give *o* or *ŭ* other than their current English sounds. *Ejus*, for instance, was pronounced *ay-juss*, the *u* and the *j* having the sounds that they have in the English *just.* Only such variations from current English sounds were made, therefore, as were necessary to preserve medieval rhymes, and barely enough for that. The community at Downside at the time included English monks from Douai, but all used the same pronunciation. A change was introduced, however, about the year 1885, when the late Cardinal Gasquet, who was then Prior of Downside, abolished the old English pronunciation and introduced the Italian, on the plea of conformity with the practice of other communities.

The Benedictines of Ampleforth also abandoned the English pronunciation in favour of the Italian about the same time.

The old pronunciation was retained even longer at the seminary of Ushaw, where it survived until about 1898. Ushaw was a 1794 transplantation of the English College founded at Douai in 1568 by Cardinal Allen and his Oxford friends. As both Ushaw and Douai were tenacious of tradition, it would have been probable, even without supporting evidence, that the Latin pronunciation maintained at Ushaw until practically the end of the nineteenth century was the lineal descendant of the medieval English pronunciation.

The English Jesuits still use the old liturgical pronunciation, combining current English consonants with old-fashioned English vowels. Their pronunciation is identical with that used by the Benedictines of Downside until 1885, except that, early in the twentieth century, they decided to give *j* a *y* sound, and to keep *t* hard before *i*. To the English Jesuits belongs, therefore, the distinction of using the nearest equivalent of the medieval English pronunciation of Latin. A similar pronunciation is used by some of the Jesuits in the United States, if not by all of them.

If an English-speaking Jesuit is saying Mass, his accent generally makes it immediately obvious whether he is American, English, Scotch, or Irish. If, however, he were using a so-called Italian pronunciation, it would be equally easy to guess his nationality—so persistent are national differences, even in the pronunciation of Latin.

XI

Until evidence of later usage is forthcoming, we may assume that the old pronunciation of Church Latin among Roman Catholics in England had been everywhere replaced by the Italian pronunciation, except among the Jesuits, by the end of the nineteenth century.

During the whole of that century, however, opposition to the complete italianisation of "the body" had never been extinct, even among converts. Before the century closed, the opposition had decidedly the upper hand, and the resultant improvement in church architecture and furniture would have delighted Pugin. There was even a reaction against the Italian pronunciation of liturgical Latin. This reaction, although it has apparently lasted in only one place to the present time, is nevertheless of interest, particularly as it was due, at least indirectly, to the influence of "Mother Damnable".

During the last quarter of the nineteenth century, relations between the English adherents of Rome and Canterbury became less bitter than they had been. When the excitement caused by the first secessions from Tractarianism had subsided, those who stayed behind took Keble's injunction to heart, and spoke more gently than they had done of their sister's fall. Conversions to Rome, too, became so numerous that the feelings aroused by them on both sides could not maintain their earlier intensity. As a result, there was less talk of the Scarlet Woman, and no more talk of Mother Damnable. The sons of the converts, moreover, were hereditary Roman Catholics, and therefore did not suffer from the inferiority-complex of their fathers.

Consequently, not only was there less tendency to italianisation, but there was even a tendency to copy Anglican ways in some respects—a tendency which has not yet spent its force.

While it would be absurd to claim that Roman Catholics in England have copied Anglicans to anything approaching the extent that Anglicanism has copied Rome, the copying has not been entirely in one direction. The peculiarly Anglican art of change-ringing, for instance—evolved by Anglicanism in its most Protestant eighteenth-century days—has been introduced into more than one Roman Catholic belfry. The gaiters, apron, and top-hat inherited by the Anglican bishops of to-day from their predecessors of the same period, now decorate the person of more than one member of the Roman Catholic hierarchy. The restraint noticeable in the furnishing of many Roman Catholic churches can scarcely escape the charge of owing something to Anglican influence, nor can the care bestowed on music in their cathedrals.

Another cause of the growth of a kindlier feeling between Anglicanism and Roman Catholicism was the abolition of religious tests at the old universities in 1871. Though Oxford and Cambridge remained—as they still remain—predominantly Anglican in membership and tone, the Pope in 1895 allowed his subjects to enter them, and a number of hereditary Roman Catholics took advantage of this permission to share in the advantages of a Protestant education.

By this time, a new pronunciation of Latin had arisen in England. This was the reformed pronunciation of Classical Latin, formulated about 1870 by Oxford and Cambridge scholars, mostly Anglican clergymen, who re-converted Cicero, long called Sisero, into Kikero.

The new pronunciation made little headway at first, and encountered an opposition which is far from dead yet. Those who adopted it, however, did so whole-heartedly. Among them was a section of the Roman Catholic clergy, some of whom perhaps obtained it from printed sources, others, no doubt, from direct contact with it at Oxford or Cambridge.

Wherever they acquired the new pronunciation, there was certainly a group of Roman Catholic clergy who, about the beginning of the twentieth century, had the greatest enthusiasm for it. They did not share St Jerome's fear that Ciceronianism spelled damnation. On the contrary, their enthusiasm for the classics was so great that they introduced the new pronunciation into a sphere for which it was in some respects ill-fitted, and which its originators had not taken into consideration. At one bound, they leaped over the "chees and chaws" and the "*Garden-of-the-Soul* Catholics". Pausing to make a respectful bow to Urban VIII, Pius V, and Erasmus, they took another leap over the Middle Ages, the Dark Ages, St Jerome himself, and shook the great writers of pagan Rome warmly by the hand— for these were the men whose pronunciation was now to be used in the recitation of the Missal and Breviary. Thus, not merely the quantitative hymns of Renaissance and later writers, with their appropriate references to *Olympus* and *tartara,* but also the rhythmical, rhymed verses of St Thomas Aquinas, Thomas of Celano, and Giacopone da Todi, with their homely, half-Romance vocabulary, were sung to the accents of Virgil, Horace, and Cicero.

Among those who adopted this innovation was that most attractive liturgiologist, Dr Adrian Fortescue, who introduced it into his church at Letchworth. It appears to have survived there until his death in 1923, but has been abandoned since then, in favour of the Italian pronunciation.

The new pronunciation was also used by some, though not all, of the clergy of Westminster Cathedral in 1903. Its use was never officially adopted there, neither did it survive very long. One priest, however, who heard it there has the clearest recollection of its effect on him. He had been brought up on the Italian pronunciation, and had not come in contact with the classical pronunciation before. Consequently, when he heard some of the clergy singing *in sighcula sigh-culorum*, instead of *in saycula sayculorum*, his first impression was that this must be a Cockney pronunciation, and he expected to hear them say *lidy* for *lady*.

This new ecclesiastical pronunciation, however, does not appear to have spread very far, or to have lasted very long in Roman Catholic churches in England, except in one place, where it survives to the present day.

This is at the Benedictine abbey of Ampleforth, where it supplanted the Italian pronunciation about twenty years ago. Its introduction there was probably influenced by the existence of a public school in connection with the abbey. It is obviously confusing to schoolboys if they hear one pronunciation of Latin in school and another in church. Downside has solved the problem—though its method of solving it has given rise to another—by using the Italian pronunciation for the teaching of the classics. Ampleforth has solved it by using the classical pronunciation both scholastically and liturgically.

The difficulty, so often lamented by schoolmasters, of teaching the classical pronunciation to schoolboys must be most acute in Roman Catholic schools where the Italian pronunciation is used liturgically. Even in Anglican schools, where Latin is seldom or never heard in chapel, a boy has to acquire his grasp of the classical pronunciation from the lips of his Classics master. At Ampleforth, however, he has unique opportunities, for he hears Latin not merely spoken, but also sung, with the classical pronunciation, and it comes, not from one man, but from a whole body of monks.

In a parish church, on the other hand, with a congregation composed of educated and uneducated persons, and with a single-handed priest to instruct them, the teaching of the classical pronunciation is exceptionally difficult. Even Dr Fortescue must have found it so. Still, he was used to difficult positions, being a Jacobite in politics.

XII

Considering that the introduction of "chees and chaws" was merely one feature of a wide movement for italianising Roman Catholicism in England, and considering the extent to which the italianisation of the Church of England also has gone, it will be of interest to see what progress, if any, the Italian pronunciation of Latin has made in the more limited field available for it within the comprehensive walls of the latter.

Anglican places of worship which use any Latin in their services fall into two clearly defined groups of very different character. The first group consists of cathedrals, collegiate churches, and the chapels of university colleges and public schools.

In all of these, the liturgical use of Latin has, for certain purposes, an unbroken tradition since the Reformation. It was definitely allowed at the universities by the Act of Uniformity of 1549, by the authorisation of a Latin translation of the Book of Common Prayer in 1560, and by the Act of Uniformity of 1662. The latter Act allows the use of Latin at all services "in the Chapels or other Publick Places of the respective Colleges and Halls in both the Universities, in the Colledges of Westminster, Winchester, and Eaton, and in the Convocations of the Clergies of either Province".

If, therefore, all the services in these places were in Latin, they would be quite legal, even from the Erastian point of view. Further, the first Act of Uniformity, which limited the privilege to the chapels of the university colleges, decidedly encourages the holding in them of services in Greek, Latin, or Hebrew, "for the further encouraging of learning in the tongues".

In practice, however, Latin is not used for a whole service, except on a few occasions in cathedrals. Even there, it is used only at services of a semi-private character for the clergy, such as at the opening of Convocation, when even the sermon is in Latin. At such services as the installation of a dean or canon, Latin is partly used, perhaps wholly so in some cathedrals. In general, however, it is used in cathedrals and college chapels only for the singing of an occasional hymn or anthem.

Until very recently, these were the only places where any Latin was used in the Anglican rite. The clergy who used it were, consequently, in that sense a small religious minority. Might they not, therefore, like the Roman Catholic clergy, have retained something of the pronunciation of an earlier period in their liturgical Latin?

There were two things which militated against that. First of all, Latin was used in Anglican cathedrals and college chapels only occasionally —too seldom to exercise a retarding effect on phonetic changes. Secondly, the clergy who used it, or who supervised its use by choirs, were drawn almost entirely from the old universities. Accustomed as they were to the academic pronunciation of Latin, which followed the gradual changes of English speech, they must almost inevitably have used the same pronunciation on such few occasions as they used Latin liturgically. It may be taken as practically certain, therefore, that, in all Anglican cathedrals and college chapels, the custom from the Reformation onwards was to pronounce Latin, both vowels and consonants, like current English.

So the custom continued until late in the nine-teenth century, when the reformed pronuncia-tion of Classical Latin was introduced into academic circles. The connection between the university lecture-room on the one hand and the college chapel and the cathedral on the other was so close that the new pronunciation inevitably found its way into Anglican liturgical usage, even though liturgical Latin is not Classical Latin. But, just as the reformed pronunciation has not yet ousted the old entirely from the lecture-room, neither has it done so from the college chapels or the cathedrals. Some use the old pronunciation, some the new.

A third pronunciation, in which English consonant-sounds are combined with Continental vowel-sounds, is also used here and there—in St George's Chapel, Windsor, for instance. This pronunciation is identical with that at which the Roman Catholics aimed before they were outsung by converts from Anglicanism. Its use must probably be regarded, however, not as a liturgical survival, but as a recent, though welcome and soundly practical innovation.

The Italian pronunciation does not appear to have made much headway in Anglican cathedrals or college chapels up to the present. There are, however, at least two college chapels into which the "chees and chaws" which annoyed the hereditary Roman Catholics about the middle of the nineteenth century have recently been introduced and can be heard whenever a Latin hymn or a Christmas carol with a Latin refrain is sung.

There is every reason to believe that this innovation was not due to deliberate Faberism. It was probably due to the influence of travels in Italy, of wireless programmes, and of choral societies which base their pronunciation on well-known manuals for singers.

It is nevertheless identical with the Faberian pronunciation, so that Faberism has gained a footing even in those academic strongholds of "Mother Damnable" which it abandoned long ago as impossible. It will be interesting to see how the movement progresses in this quarter. It will probably grow, because a service of attractive popular character, including some Latin, is broadcast at intervals from one of the two chapels in question.

On the whole, however, Anglican cathedrals and college chapels have not yet been italianised, whether in ornamentation or in Latin pronunciation. They stand, in these matters, more or less where the Roman Catholics stood in the early years of the nineteenth century.

XIII

The second group of Anglican places of worship in which any Latin is used consists of a few parish churches, together with the chapels of one or two religious communities.

The use of Latin in parish churches is of recent introduction, and is contrary, not merely to the Act of Uniformity, but also to the whole tradition of Anglicanism. To its introducers, however, these considerations are of no weight—or rather, they are not reasons against the use of Latin, but reasons for it. To them, the first half of the word "Anglo-Catholic" is a rock of offence; for "Catholic" is to them, as to the Faberians, synonymous with "Roman".

The amount of Latin used by the members of this group varies from place to place. In the religious communities in question, the whole of every service is in Latin. In the parish churches, a whole service may be in Latin, or the only Latin used may be a litany, an *Adoremus in aeternum* at the service of Benediction, an *Agnus Dei* at the Eucharist, or a mere *Ite, missa est* sung before the blessing. In one church, a cleric with a very limited knowledge of Latin used a few years ago to content himself with interlarding his sermons with frequent quotations from the Vulgate.

However much the proportion of Latin to English may vary in the churches of this group, the pronunciation, as far as the present writer's experience goes, is always the same. As one would expect, it is an attempt at the Italian pronunciation, "with an extreme Roman accent". Yet, whether it be from ignorance, or from some dreg of Anglicanism stirring in the depths of the subconscious mind, it is generally described as "the ecclesiastical pronunciation". All discussion is thereby silenced, as effectively as when one adherent of this group, when asked to justify a sermon on the miracles of some saint, quoted the statements of the Roman Breviary as conclusive evidence.

XIV

It is not surprising to hear the "chees and chaws" pronunciation in an Anglican parish church where "Acts of Reparation for the 'Reformation'"—though it provided the vicar with a wife —are regularly performed. Neither is it surprising to hear it in a church where a side-chapel is decorated with the text *Verbum caro factus* (sic) *est*, and where the restored local shrine—the restoration is dated by the year of the reigning Pope—is proudly described in the church porch as "England's Santa Cassa" (sic). What is surprising is to hear the "chees and chaws" in college chapels, particularly in one of them which is associated with one of the finest defences of Anglicanism published in recent years.

It cannot be maintained that no other pronunciation is suited to singing. The Spaniards, for instance, get on very well without it. On the rare occasions when a Spanish cathedral choir rises to the artistic level of an English village choir, the result is as pleasing to the ear as if an Italian choir were performing.

Can it be said that the *Te Deum*, or St Ambrose's

> *Splendor paternae gloriae,*
> *De luce lucem proferens,*
> *Lux lucis et fons luminis*

lose anything in majesty or beauty if deprived of "chees and chaws"? It would be strange if it were so, seeing that those sounds were not evolved until after the authors of these two hymns were dead. Can it be maintained that the immortal *Rosy Sequence* loses any of its haunting charm if sung without sounds which its author did not use?

Reasonable objections may be raised to a pronunciation based on English consonants and current English vowels, and practical objections can certainly be raised to the liturgical use of the reformed classical pronunciation.

64

The latter is, naturally, well suited in spirit to the hymns of Prudentius and other early writers, and to post-Renaissance hymns, with their strictly metrical forms, but is not so suited to the accentual hymns of St Thomas Aquinas and other medieval writers.

There is also the difficulty of rhymes. The reformed classical pronunciation differentiates sharply between the sounds of short vowels and the corresponding long vowels. In medieval hymns, on the other hand, as in earlier rhymed hymns, long vowels rhyme with short ones, and *e* rhymes with *ae*. In the earlier writers—Venantius Fortunatus, for instance—this does not matter so much, as their rhyme is but sporadic and plays no important part. In the medieval hymns, on the other hand, rhymes occur in every line, and are a feature of the highest importance in the general effect.

The classical pronunciation, in fact, not only does not pretend to cater for Medieval Latin, but is also inapplicable to it. To quote but one example, it eliminates the rhymes from

> *Recordare, Jesu pie,*
> *Quod sum causa tuae viae;*
> *Ne me perdas illa die.*[1]

[1] The number of hymns and sequences in the current Roman Missal and Breviary in which the rhymes are effaced by using the reformed classical pronunciation is,

The unsuitability of both the old academic English pronunciation and the reformed classical pronunciation need not, nevertheless, drive educated English choirs to sing *Gloria in eck-shell-cease*—or *ex-chell-cease*, as is sometimes heard. There still remains the via media of using English consonants with vowels of a modified Continental type, corresponding to the vowels of earlier English, before their letters had switched over to their present sounds.

The use of a pronunciation of this kind would retain, as far as is possible, the old principle of pronouncing liturgical Latin like the vernacular. It has all the practical advantages of the Italian pronunciation without its complexity or its alien taint. It also makes Latin more intelligible to the ordinary Englishman.

The fact that nearly all the consonants would be identical with French ones is an additional argument in its favour, for the French and Franco-Latin elements in the English language are very great. Further, millions of Englishmen now know some French, whereas not one Englishman in ten thousand knows any Italian.

The Italian language does not, as is sometimes

however, surprisingly small. Of the 170 or so compositions in the two books, only 15 are in regular rhyme, and in only 7 of these is the rhyme spoiled if the reformed pronunciation is used.

imagined, come almost automatically to the person who knows a moderate amount of Latin, or even to the Latin scholar. Still less does its pronunciation do so, and this is particularly true of the vowels.

Italian pronunciation is not merely, or even primarily, a matter of "chees and chaws", even though these are what first strike the ear of those who are unfamiliar with the language. The vowels are the important factor, and Italian vowels are unnatural to English lips. A list of "simple rules" for acquiring an Italian pronunciation of Latin, culled from a musical handbook, may provide a fair guide for the consonants; but, for the vowels, it is of about as much use as the "imitated pronunciation" given in a *Hottentot Self-taught* manual would be for acquiring a Hottentot pronunciation.

Before attempting to teach the singing of Latin in the Italian style, the choir-trainer himself should be able to sing with a decent Italian accent. Yet, even in university towns in England, there are very few persons who can do so. The result is that English attempts to sing Latin with an Italian pronunciation often produce nothing but a parody, like that produced by superior persons who, scorning the honest English "Marsails" for "Marseille", imagine that they are speaking French when they call it "Mah-say".

In any event, the pronunciation of *magna* as *mah-nyah* is out of place in a country where "Magna" is a common adjunct to place-names. So is the pronunciation of *crucifixus* as *cruchifixus* in a country familiar with the word "crucifix". A pronunciation based on current English consonants and old-fashioned English vowels, on the other hand, would not clash with the principles of the English language, and would make English etymology, and incidentally French etymology, clearer to the ordinary person. It would be readily understood by Frenchmen, Germans, and Spaniards, and would be as intelligible to Italians as the present so-called Italian pronunciation. Such a pronunciation has a long English tradition behind it, and could even put forward a claim to being the old English pronunciation.

"God forbid", says a well-known Roman Catholic writer of to-day, "that we should try to make devotion into a highbrow exercise.... Church Latin was not meant to mystify. It was meant to express, not to conceal."

INDEX

INDEX

www.ingramcontent.com/pod-product-compliance
Ingram Content Group UK Ltd.
Pitfield, Milton Keynes, MK11 3LW, UK
UKHW020447010325
455719UK00015B/468